Girl! *What you gonna DO with your* MONEY?

Money Matters for Kids

For Girls (ages 5 to 12)

Ti'Juana Gholson

illustrator: **Trevor Lucas**

Published in the United States of America.
ISBN: 13: 978-1-970097-07-8
Book cover and body illustrations by Trevor Lucas – Anomaly, LLC

Published by:
MAX Publishing, LLC

How do I feel about Money?

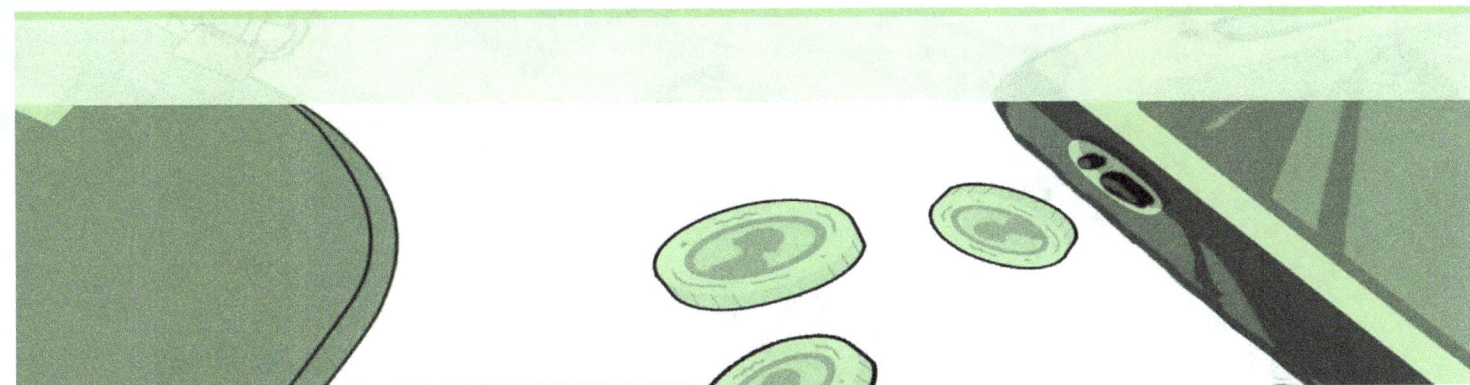

I LIKE Money!

Money makes me feel HAPPY!!

I can buy things with Money!

My parents pay the bills with Money!

Money makes the world go around.

How do I feel about Money?

_____

_____

_____

_____

_____

_____

What can I buy with Money?

_____
_____
_____
_____

What do I see my parents buy with Money?

_____
_____
_____
_____

BANK

2

How to Save Money

Ti' gets an allowance for doing chores.

Ti' makes a purchase.

Ti' saves her change.

Ti' puts it in a jar.

Ti' keeps it in a safe place.

Once Ti' has a lot saved, her mom takes her to the bank to deposit it.

Ti's Money grows in interest.

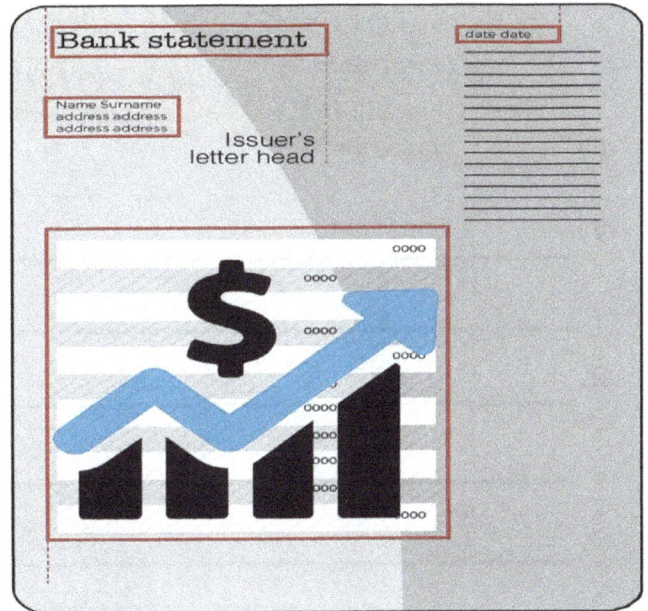

Ti' is happy.

Write 3 ways you can save the Money you get for your birthday, for doing chores, for jobs like walking dogs and for doing little things around the house.

1. _____

_____

2. _____

_____

3. _____

_____

3

Work for your Money

Ti' works.

Ti' gets her paycheck.

Dairy King

DATE

0000

PAY TO THE ORDER OF Ti' Gholson

Two Hundred Dollars

$ 200.00

DOLLARS

MEMO

⑆0⑈234356789⑆ 0⑈234356789⑈ ⑈234

Ti' budgets her Money.

Ti' pays her bills!

CREDIT REPORT

785

A+

The people she owes
Money give her an
A on her credit
report card!

Ti' does well with her Money!

List 3 ways that you can budget and pay your bills:

1. _____

_____

2. _____

_____

3. _____

_____

Discuss with an adult.

FINANCIAL FREEDOM

→

4

Be FREE with your Money:

Financial Freedom Free to be ME!

Ti' saved money.

Ti' has ideas!

LEMONADE

$1 CUPS

Ti' has Money
coming in
from her ideas.

Ti' doesn't have to be at work or at a job to make Money!

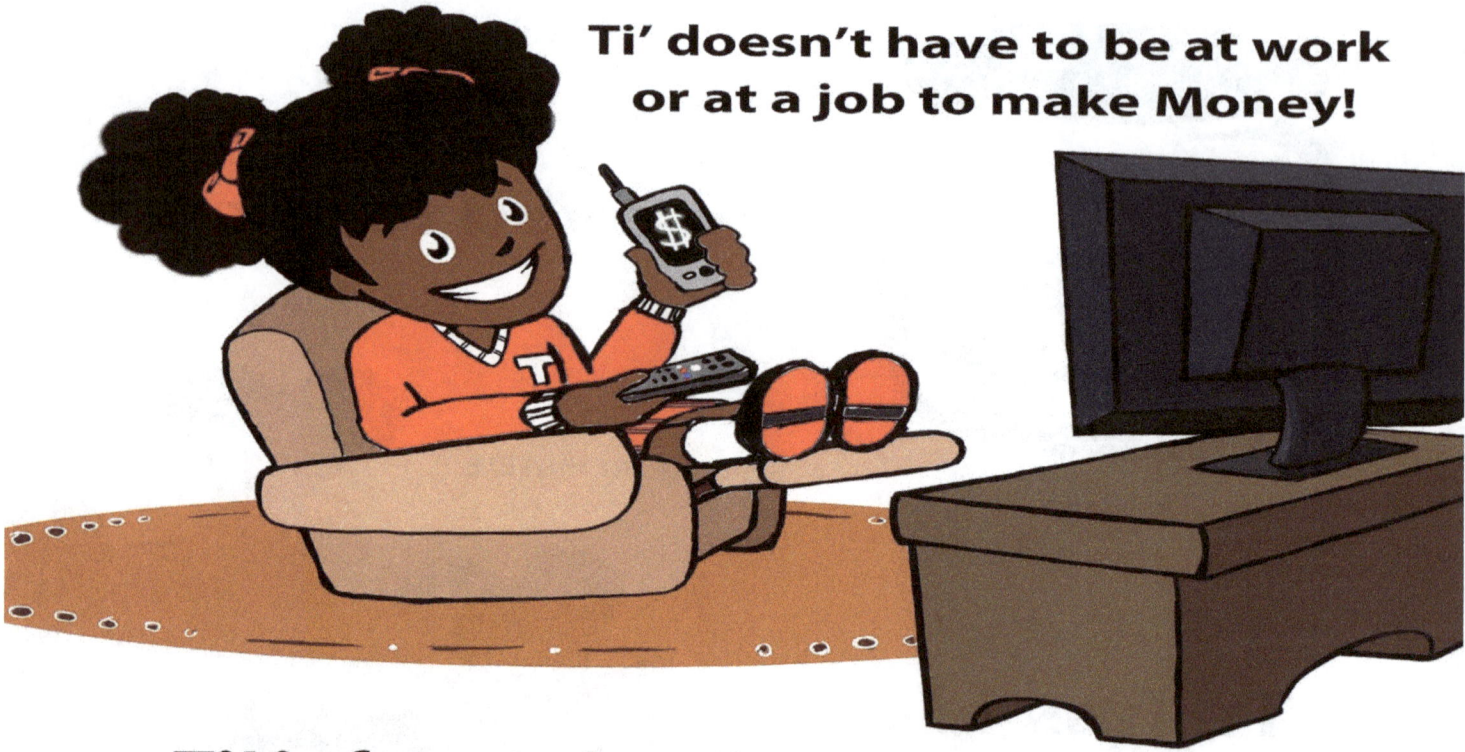

Ti' is free to be Ti'!

Lesson:

1. What do you like to do? Write ways that you can make Money without having a job.

2. Talk with an adult about ways that you can make Money with your creative ideas.

List your ideas.

1. _____

2. _____

3. _____

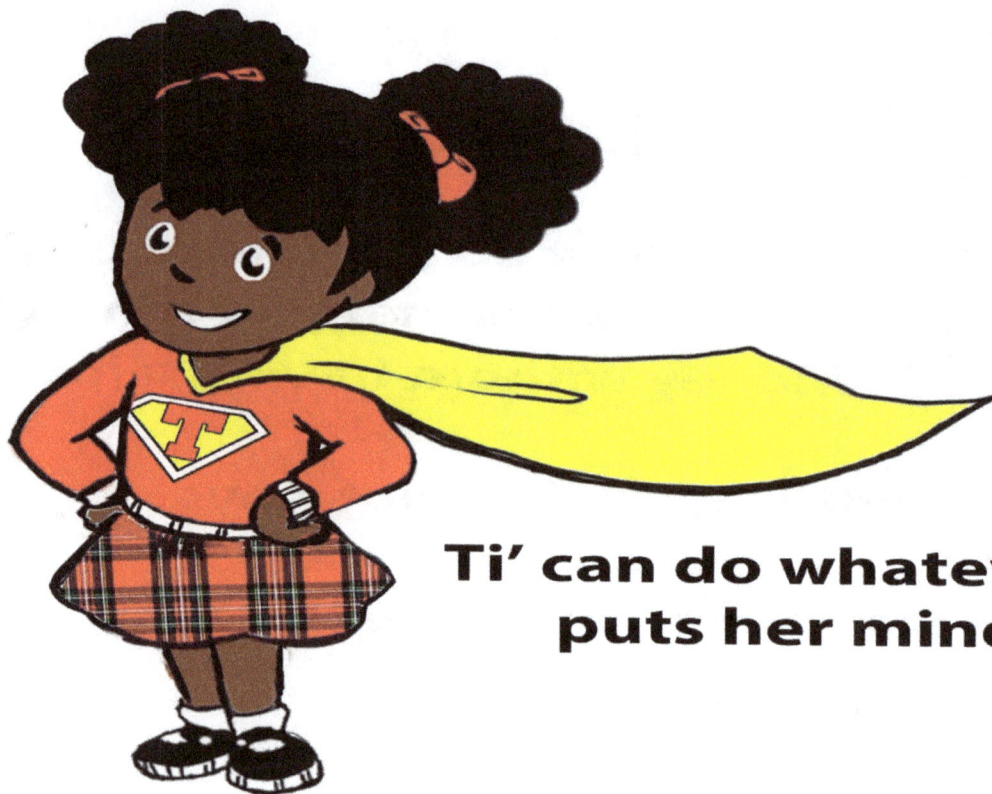

Ti' can do whatever she puts her mind to!

Ti' got started and so can you!

Ti' talks to adults!

Ti' talks to her parents!

Ti' talks to her teachers!

Ti' knows a lot about money and now . . .

. . . so do you!

Only one question remains:

What are you going to do with YOUR Money?

www.ingramcontent.com/pod-product-compliance
Lightning Source LLC
Chambersburg PA
CBHW081750200326
41597CB00024B/4456

9 781970 097078